Powers of the Mind

Brian Innes

RSVP

RAINTREE
STECK-VAUGHN
PUBLISHERS
A Steck-Vaughn Company

Austin, Texas

www.steck-vaughn.com

Developed by Brown Partworks
Editor: Lindsey Lowe
Designer: Joan Curtis
Picture Researcher: Brigitte Arora

Raintree Steck-Vaughn Publishers Staff
Project Manager: Joyce Spicer
Editor: Pam Wells

Library of Congress Cataloging-in-Publication Data
Innes, Brian.
    Powers of the mind/by Brian Innes.
        p.   cm.—(Unsolved mysteries)
    Includes bibliographical references and index.
    Summary: Recounts instances of telepathy, telekinesis, clairvoyance, and
other paranormal events and suggests possible explanations for them.
    ISBN 0-8172-5488-9 (Hardcover)
    ISBN 0-8172-5850-7 (Softcover)
    1. Extrasensory perception—Juvenile literature. [1. Estrasensory perception.]
I. Title. II. Series: Innes, Brian. Unsolved mysteries.
BF1321.I56   1999
133.8—dc21   98-30154
                                                        CIP
                                                        AC
Printed and bound in the United States
1 2 3 4 5 6 7 8 9 0 WZ 02 01 00 99 98

Acknowledgments

Cover: Michael Freeman/Corbis; **Page 5:** Dr. Elmar R. Gruber/Fortean Picture Library; **Page 6:** UPI/Corbis-Bettmann; **Page 7:** Hulton-Deutsch Collection/Corbis; **Page 9:** Mary Evans Picture Library; **Page 10:** UPI/Corbis-Bettmann; **Page 11:** Mary Evans Picture Library; **Page 12:** UPI/Corbis; **Page 15:** Dr. Susan Blackmore/Fortean Picture Library; **Page 16:** Dr. Elmar R. Gruber/Fortean Picture Library; **Page 18:** Morton Beebe-S. F./Corbis; **Page 19:** Dr. Elmar R. Gruber/Fortean Picture Library; **Page 21:** Nils Jorgensen/Rex Features; **Page 22:** Harry Price Collection/University of London/Mary Evans Picture Library; **Page 23:** Guy Lyon Playfair/Fortean Picture Library; **Page 24:** UPI/Corbis; **Page 26:** Manfred Cassirer/Mary Evans Picture Library; **Page 27:** Society for Psychical Research/Mary Evans Picture Library; **Page 29:** Mark Gibson/Corbis; **Page 30:** UPI/Corbis-Bettmann; **Page 32:** Mary Evans Picture Library; **Page 35:** Library of Congress/Corbis; **Page 36:** Hulton-Deutsch Collection/Corbis; **Page 37:** Jim Sugar Photography/Corbis; **Page 38:** Roger Ressmeyer/Corbis; **Page 39:** Vittoriano Rastelli/Corbis; **Page 41:** Dr. Elmar R. Gruber/Fortean Picture Library; **Page 42:** Mary Evans Picture Library; **Page 43:** Richard Megna/Fundamental/Science Photo Library; **Page 44:** Image Factory/Explorer/Science Photo Library; **Page 45:** Dennis Stacy/Fortean Picture Library; **Page 46:** Richard T. Nowitz/Corbis.

Contents

Messages in the Mind

This picture (opposite), titled The Aura, was painted by Ingo Swann. An aura is said to be a misty glow that surrounds people. Swann and other people with unusual powers of the mind claim to be able to see a person's aura.

Ingo Swann, an American artist, sat in a room in New York. A solid platform hung several feet above his head. Colored drawings and paintings had been placed on top of the platform. Swann could not see them from where he was sitting. He was making sketches of any pictures that came into his mind. The sketches, and notes about their colors that Swann wrote beside them, were amazingly like the drawings and paintings on the platform.

A SIXTH SENSE

Swann was taking part in an experiment. The experiment was being done by the American Society for Psychical Research. Members of the society are interested in powers of the mind that do not have any scientific explanation—at least, at present. The powers are often grouped together under the name extrasensory perception (ESP). They are called "extrasensory" because people who have these powers seem to use something other than the five human senses—sight, touch, hearing, smell, and taste. Some people think that humans also have a sixth sense—or perhaps even more!

4

Swann was making sketches of any pictures that came into his mind.

There are several possible explanations for Swann's success in the experiments. At least one of the scientists in the room would have been able to see the pictures on the platform. Swann might have been able to "tune into," or link up with, the other person's thoughts. This kind of ESP is known as telepathy.

A television camera was used to film the experiments, so Swann might have been able to see the pictures as they were recorded. Or perhaps, in some way, he could actually "see" them in his mind. This is called clairvoyance, from the French word meaning "clear seeing."

Ophelia Rivers, a scientist at Mississippi State University, carried out ESP tests on twins in the 1960s. One of the tests (above) was something like the Ingo Swann experiments. Here one twin is holding a card. She "tells" her sister what is on the card using telepathy. According to Rivers, the test was a success.

Swann's own explanation was quite different. He claimed that he went into a kind of sleeplike state. Then he felt his mind float up to the ceiling, look at the pictures on the platform, and return again to his body. This type of happening is known as "remote viewing." *Remote* is a word that describes something that is at a distance, or is operated or controlled from a distance. In his case, Swann said he was able to look at the pictures without moving from his seat.

SCIENTIFIC STUDIES

The study of a happening such as Swann's, which cannot be explained by normal science, is called parapsychology. For centuries most people believed in such ESP experiences. In many parts of the world, people still do, particularly in Eastern countries. However, during the 19th century scientists in the West began to laugh at such ideas. They thought that anything they could not explain could not have happened. They said people claiming to have had ESP experiences were just fooling themselves.

In some cases, these scientists were certainly right. But there were many other cases that could not be explained away. As a result a number of people got together and founded societies, or groups, for psychical research. "Psychic" is from the ancient Greek word *psyche* and means "of or in the mind." The first modern word using this meaning was "psychology." These groups included many scientists who were interested in finding reasons for such things as telepathy, clairvoyance, and remote viewing.

The first of these societies was the National Society for Psychical Research, set up in London in 1882. The American branch was started five years later. Since then many similar societies have been set up all over the world.

MEETING AT THE STATION

An Englishwoman named Rosalind Heywood was a famous psychical researcher. She wrote a book titled *The Infinite Hive*. In the book, Heywood described her experiences of telepathy. One of the stories she told was about a day in

This is the National Society for Psychical Research in London, England. It was set up in 1882.

7

1944. It was during World War II. Her husband was a soldier, and he was expected home on leave. His train was due to arrive at 8:00 P.M.

Mrs. Heywood lay down for a rest at 6:30 P.M. However, after only ten minutes she suddenly felt that she had to telephone the railroad station. She was told that her husband's train would arrive an hour earlier than expected. Then she had a strong feeling that her husband wanted her to meet him at the station, with a porter ready to carry his bags.

So, while he was on the train, he had tried to send her a message using telepathy.

Mrs. Heywood rushed to the station and found a porter. When the train arrived, her husband was amazed to see her. He told her that he had not been able to phone her before getting on his train because there were long lines of people waiting to use the telephones. So, while he was on the train, he had tried to send her a message using telepathy. Amazingly, she had received it!

HIDDEN TALENT

Pearl Curran was from St. Louis, Missouri. She had a very different kind of experience. One day in 1913, Mrs. Curran began to write poetry. She said the poetry came to her as messages. She claimed the messages had been put into her mind by a person named Patience Worth. Mrs. Curran said Patience was a girl who had lived in the 17th century.

Mrs. Curran spoke Patience's messages aloud. Her husband wrote them down. Between 1913 and 1937, Pearl Curran produced thousands of poems, seven full-length historical novels, plays, and many other writings. Many were published, and the books were read by people throughout the United States.

Professor Charles Cory of Washington University, St. Louis, Missouri, tried to explain how Mrs. Curran could have written what she did. He said that she had simply been keeping her talent a secret until 1913. But Walter Franklin Price of the American Society for Psychical Research did not agree. Pearl Curran had only a basic education and was not interested in history or novels. He said it was impossible for Mrs. Curran to have known the historical facts that she put in her novels. As for Mrs. Curran herself, she honestly believed that the messages came to her from a girl called Patience.

Mr. and Mrs. Coates (above) carrying out a test along the lines of the Ossowiecki experiment. She is "reading" what is written on the paper inside a sealed envelope.

SECRET WRITING

The National Society for Psychical Research in London carried out many amazing experiments in clairvoyance. One involved a Polish engineer named Stefan Ossowiecki.

Two tests were done. In each case, a drawing was made on a sheet of paper. Some words were written underneath the drawing. The paper was

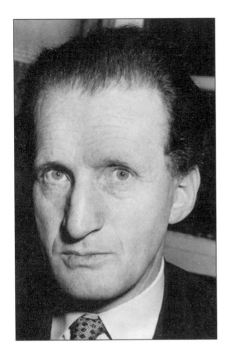

This is Gerald Croiset. He and his son became famous for solving crime cases using their powers of telepathy.

folded and put into an envelope. Then the envelope was put inside another envelope. This envelope was put inside a third envelope. This meant that there was no way of seeing what was inside the first envelope. The complete package was secretly marked, so that scientists would know if it had been opened by anyone.

The package was given to Ossowiecki by a person who had no idea what was inside it. Ossowiecki was then asked to draw what was inside the sealed envelope. The first drawing was a large, tall bottle. Ossowiecki drew it exactly. He could not make out the writing under the drawing. However, he said he thought it was in French. This was true. The second drawing was of a small bottle of ink. Ossowiecki drew a small ink bottle and wrote "SWAN INK." Unbelievably, this was totally correct!

WHO OWNED IT? WHERE DID IT COME FROM?

A particular kind of clairvoyance is known as psychometry. People with this power hold an object in their hands. They can then explain who owned it or where it had come from. One of the most famous people with this ability was a Dutchman named Gerald Croiset. In the 1940s and 1950s, the Dutch police often asked Croiset to help them solve crimes or find missing people. His son, Gerald Croiset, Jr., also had the same powers.

DOWSING

Another strange form of ESP is known as dowsing. For centuries, people have used dowsing to find underground water supplies. The traditional way of dowsing is to hold a forked stick of hazelwood between the two hands. As the user walks across a piece of land, the stick jerks and bends whenever it passes over the site of an underground spring, well, or stream.

More modern dowsing methods include the use of copper strips, or even a piece of bent wire. In some cases a small weight is hung from a thread that is then held between the thumb and first finger. Some dowsers do nothing more than simply hang such a weight over a map. They claim that just by doing this they know where water, oil, or minerals are to be found. Dowsers have also found lost objects.

In 1913, this illustration appeared in a French magazine, Le Petit Journal. *It shows a successful dowsing demonstration that had been held near Paris.*

Exercising the Mind

Over the years, all kinds of tests have been done on people with ESP. Some of the results have been amazing.

In 1930 the American writer Upton Sinclair published a book titled *Mental Radio*. In it, Sinclair told the stories of some 290 different experiments in telepathy that he had carried out with his wife. Mary Craig Sinclair suffered from severe pain due to sickness. However, she had learned to control the pain by using special mental exercises. She was able to clear her mind and relax completely.

DRAWN FROM THE MIND

Over a few years, Mrs. Sinclair had become friendly with a young man named Jan. She found that she knew exactly what he was doing, even when he was far away.

One day, Mrs. Sinclair wrote about something she had dreamed. She said that Jan had come to visit her in her dream. He had brought her a small basket of violets and pink roses. She drew the basket of flowers. The next day she received a letter from Jan. He had cut slits in the paper and pushed the stems of violets and pink cosmos into them. The shape the flowers made on the paper was like the basket that Mrs. Sinclair had drawn the day before.

Upton Sinclair in his study in 1934. (opposite). His book, Mental Radio, listed nearly 300 examples of his wife's amazing telepathic powers.

12

"I don't like to believe in telepathy, because I don't know what to make of it. "

UPTON SINCLAIR

Upton Sinclair decided to test his wife's telepathic ability. He sat in his study with the door shut. Then he drew anything that came into his mind. Several rooms away, his wife tried to draw the same picture. The drawings were mostly simple shapes, but some, such as animals or human figures, were more difficult. Sometimes Mrs. Sinclair would add words to describe what she was trying to draw.

Mary Sinclair thought hard and then wrote, "See a table fork, nothing else."

Some of Mrs. Sinclair's drawings were almost exactly what her husband had drawn. Others were only parts of the original. For example, Sinclair drew a deer with huge branching antlers. His wife drew the branches, but underneath she wrote "holly leaves." And when Sinclair drew a steamboat, she drew only the smokestack with smoke coming out of it. Upton Sinclair asked his secretary and his brother to take part in some more tests.

One day, Mary Craig Sinclair's brother-in-law was 40 miles (64 km) away in Pasadena, California. He drew a picture of a fork. At the same time, Mary Sinclair thought hard and then wrote, "See a table fork, nothing else."

Of the 290 drawings, the Sinclairs said 65 were completely successful, 155 (such as the deer and holly) were partly successful, and 70 were failures. Upton Sinclair took the results seriously, but one of his friends wrote a humorous newspaper article titled

"Sinclair Goes Spooky." Sinclair replied: "I don't like to believe in telepathy, because I don't know what to make of it. . . . In short, there isn't a thing in the world that leads me to this act except the conviction [belief] that has been forced upon me that telepathy is real. . . ."

OTHER TESTS

More recently, tests like Upton Sinclair's have been developed into a scientific study. The person who is being tested sits in a comfortable chair, or lies down, in a room with the door closed. Headphones over the person's ears play white noise—which is a hissing sound, something like the sound of an untuned radio. White goggles are placed over the eyes. A red lamp is shone on the goggles so that, if the person's

This is a model of a scientific ESP test. The pictures are what the woman has been asked to describe. In a real experiment, the pictures would be in another room with a scientist. The person being tested then uses a microphone to tell the scientist what he or she is seeing.

15

eyes are open, all that he or she sees is a pleasant pink light. In this relaxed state, the person is able to concentrate completely on the images that come into his or her mind. There is a microphone in the room, so that the person can tell the scientists what he or she is "seeing."

The person sending the images or pictures sits in another room. It is soundproof, so that no outside sounds can be heard inside and no inside sounds can be heard outside. A number of different images are stored on a computer. The computer chooses any one of the images and shows it on its screen. There is no way that any of the scientists know what the image will be before it comes up on the screen. A scientist then concentrates on the image. If the test is successful, the person being tested sees the same image.

This experiment has pro-duced successful results time after time. One scientist has worked out that the chance of the results being produced by accident is 1 in 10 billion.

TRAVELS IN THE MIND

Different experiments have been tried at the Stanford Research Institute. This is a leading science laboratory at Menlo Park, California, not far from San Francisco.

The first tests were with Patrick H. Price. He was a retired police commissioner

Dr. Russell Targ. In the 1970s, Targ worked at the Stanford Research Institute, where he studied people who had unusual powers of the mind.

from Burbank. Price said that during his career with the police department, he had often used the remote viewing method to catch criminals.

DETECTIVE WORK

During the 1970s Russell Targ and Hal Puthoff, two young scientists, put Price's powers to the test. One day in 1974, Puthoff got into a car with Dr. Bonnar Cox. At 3:00 P.M., they began to drive around, with no planned destination. Meanwhile Targ sat in the laboratory with Price and a tape recorder. Targ explained that Puthoff and Cox would reach a destination at 3:30 P.M. Then Price should describe where they were.

Price said . . . he had often used the remote viewing method to catch criminals.

At 3:06 P.M., Price spoke: "We don't have to wait till then. I can tell you right now where they will be. What I'm looking at is a little boat jetty, or a little boat dock along the bay. I see some motor launches [small motorboats], some little sailing ships. Sails all furled. . . . Funny thing—this just flashed in, a definite feeling of [Eastern] architecture that seems to be". . . close by.

Twenty minutes later, Puthoff and Cox pulled off the road at the Redwood City Marina. It was a harbor and boat dock about 4 miles (6.5 km) from the laboratory. Small sailboats and motorboats were tied up there. Nearby was a Chinese restaurant.

To be sure that Price had not arranged the destination with Cox and Puthoff, another test was carried out. This time, one of the scientists was given a list of 100 place-names. Without telling anybody his choices, he drove off to visit nine of them. Another scientist remained with Price. Price was asked to write down whatever entered his mind.

Price's notes were handed to a group of judges. The judges were also told the names of the nine places visited by the scientist. Then,

This is the Hoover Tower at Stanford University, Palo Alto, California. Patrick H. Price successfully named the building during a test of his telepathic powers.

they had to decide how close Price's notes were to each place visited. The best descriptions were given the number 1. In the test, Price's descriptions were numbered 1 in seven cases out of the nine. He even named one place, the Hoover Tower at Stanford.

MORE MIND TRAVELS

Sadly, Price died in 1975. However, Puthoff and Targ continued their experiments. They found a number of other remote viewers who scored even better than Price. One of them was a photographer named Hella Hammid.

In one of her first tests, Hammid successfully described five out of nine target sites. The chances of this happening were thought to be 500,000 to 1.

MESSAGES FROM THE DEEP

In July 1977, Hella Hammid was put aboard a small submarine. It was towed 2 miles (3.2 km) out to sea, just off the California coast. It then submerged, or plunged underwater. Hammid knew that one of the scientists was going to a spot somewhere in the San Francisco Bay area. But that was all she knew.

Although she suffered from seasickness, Hammid was able to correctly describe a large oak tree on a cliff overlooking Stanford University. She also said the scientist was behaving in a "very unscientific fashion." He was, in fact, climbing the oak tree!

This is Hella Hammid. In the late 1970s, she took part in a number of remote viewing tests at the Stanford Research Institute. Her powers amazed Dr. Targ.

19

Mind Over Matter

Doing something difficult is often said to be just a case of mind over matter. There is more truth in this than you might imagine!

Uri Geller was most famous for bending spoons (opposite). It has also been claimed that he could affect objects without touching them.

People who play card games regularly will tell you that if they think hard enough, they can sometimes make the cards fall as they want them to. Dice players say that they can often get the dice to show the numbers they need. But can this possibly be true? Cards and dice are lifeless objects. Most scientists say that such games are purely a matter of chance.

Nevertheless, this is an area that has attracted the attention of psychical researchers, or parapsychologists. Affecting the movement of objects without touching them is called psychokinesis (PK). This word is from an ancient Greek word, meaning "mind movement."

STRANGE FORCE

One of the earliest cases of PK to interest the American Society for Psychical Research was that of Eusapia Palladino. She was born in Italy in 1854. Her powers puzzled many scientists.

Hereward Carrington was a member of the American Society for Psychical Research. He said: "Eusapia asked me to enter the cabinet [a small space surrounded by curtains] and hold the small table within it. It was light enough

20

Millions of viewers saw Geller make metal objects bend just by stroking them.

for me to see that nothing was opposite me, even though the curtains were more or less closed. Yet some invisible being or force was strong enough to throw both the table and myself out of the cabinet completely—landing on the floor outside."

This photograph was taken in Genova, Italy, in about 1901. It shows Eusapia Palladino (center) supposedly lifting a table off the ground using PK.

NO TRICKS?

In 1894, two members of the London Society for Psychical Research visited Palladino in Italy. They said they were sure that she had some kind of mysterious power. However, Dr. Richard Hodgson, from the American Society for Psychical Research, claimed that Carrington had been tricked. Hodgson said Palladino could have used her foot to move the table.

The following year, Palladino was invited to visit England. Dr. Hodgson was also invited from the U.S. Following a number of tests, it was decided that Hodgson was right. Palladino could have used either a hand or a foot to move the table.

Thirteen years later, in 1908, members of the London Society for Psychical Research carried out more tests in Naples, Italy. Hereward Carrington was also present. This time the members decided that Palladino really did have a mysterious power that could not be explained. However, they also thought that she sometimes used tricks to achieve the results she wanted.

THE SPOON BENDER

Probably the most famous person of modern times who has claimed PK power is Uri Geller. Born in Tel Aviv, Israel, in 1946, he began his career as a nightclub entertainer. In 1972, the scientist Andrija Puharich heard about Geller and his amazing powers. He invited Geller to visit the United States.

Millions of amazed television viewers saw Geller make metal objects—such as spoons and keys—bend just by stroking them. He also claimed to be able to stop and start watches and clocks using the

special powers of his mind. Many viewers called the television studios to say that, after the program, they had found bent cutlery in their own homes. They also said that stopped watches and clocks had suddenly started up again. Geller's performances sparked a wave of interest all over the world. Many people, particularly young children, claimed that they, too, could bend cutlery.

Professor John Taylor holds a pair of bent spoons. They are souvenirs of his experiments with Uri Geller.

Two young scientists in London, England, became interested. They were John Taylor, a math professor at King's College, and John Hasted, a professor of physics at

Birkbeck College. Both set up a series of experiments to test Geller's ability. They claimed that Geller had bent a brass strip upward, using a finger pressure that was never more than half an ounce. The strip was fixed to a balance used for weighing letters so that the scientists could see how much force Geller was using.

JUST CLEVER TRICKS?

In 1975 Taylor published a book titled *Superminds*. It was about his experiments with Geller and a group of children. The book sold well. However, five years later Taylor wrote another book in which he said that Geller's powers were really tricks.

Former stage magician James Randi. After his stage career, he spent many years helping scientists to prove that some examples of psychic powers were simply clever tricks.

Hasted also wrote a book titled *The Metal Benders*. Later it was suggested that Taylor and Hasted's tests had not been set up carefully enough. James Randi, a former stage magician, said that it was easy for any good magician to produce the same results. He even went on television to prove this.

Kulagina held her hands over the compass. . . . Suddenly, the needle spun around.

Many more people came forward to say that Geller had used tricks. Others supported Geller and said he had special powers of the mind. Geller became tired by all the attention. He disappeared from public view for a number of years. Then the press reported that he had become a millionaire. Geller said he had gained his wealth by dowsing for gold and copper in distant parts of the world.

THE MYSTERY OF NINA

In Russia, then part of the Soviet Union, a woman named Nina Kulagina caused a lot of excitement among scientists in the 1960s. She was filmed using her extrasensory powers.

Before filming began, Kulagina was checked by a doctor. He had her X-rayed to be sure that she had not hidden any metal objects or magnets in her clothing. A compass was put on the table in front of her. Kulagina held her hands over the compass and thought hard about it for 20 minutes. Suddenly, the needle spun around. Then the whole compass—with

This is the psychic Nina Kulagina. In the 1960s she was filmed using her extrasensory powers. Scientists had no explanation for what happened.

its plastic case and leather strap—began to spin round and round. Kulagina leaned back, tired out.

Later a whole box of kitchen matches was scattered on a table top. Kulagina stared at them. They began to move, all together, like a log-run on a fast-flowing river. When the matches reached the edge of the table, they fell, one by one, to the floor. Another handful of matches was placed inside a large, clear plastic box. This meant that no drafts of air could move the matches. Because the box was clear, the scientists could see that no threads or wires were being used to move the matches. Kulagina passed her hands over the box and the matches began to move. They moved from one side of the box to the other.

KEEPING A SECRET

The Communist Party said that the film was not to be shown to anybody. An article in the party's newspaper, *Pravda*, stated that Kulagina was an unusual, possibly evil, person. The writer, who had actually never seen the film, went on to say that she "performs her . . . tricks with the help of magnets." It seemed that the Soviets did not want anyone to know about Nina Kulagina's mysterious powers.

RHINE'S EXPERIMENTS

Some 30 years earlier, Dr. Joseph Banks Rhine of Duke University, in Durham, North Carolina, had decided to try some experiments in psychokinesis. He chose to use dice because this was a cheap and easy way of carrying out such tests in a laboratory. He wanted to see if it was possible to use just the power of the mind to turn up particular numbers. According to the laws of chance, the right numbers would normally turn up in five guesses out of 12.

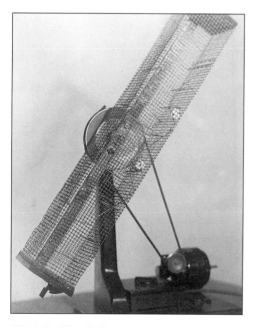

This is Dr. Rhine's dice-tumbling machine. The box was turned a number of times. When the box stopped, the dice fell to the bottom.

Rhine built a special dice-tumbling machine. A few of his students took part in the first series of 562 tests. Each one of the students was asked which numbers would show on the dice after the machine had stopped. The success rate was high. Rhine worked out that the chance of his results being produced by accident was more than 1 billion to 1!

As a result of this test, and others, Rhine thought that it was indeed possible to use the power of the mind to choose what numbers of the dice would fall uppermost.

Scientific Studies

Duke University in North Carolina (opposite). In 1927 Dr. William McDougall set up a psychology department there in order to study the mysterious powers of the mind.

Only a few scientists were in the early group of psychic researchers. Many were clergy who tried to carry out their tests so that there was no chance of being tricked. However, because they were not scientists, they did not know how to design foolproof tests.

During the 1920s, large sums of money were given to Harvard, Stanford, and Clark universities. The money came from people who wanted scientific studies of psychic happenings to be carried out. At the time there were no university departments dealing with this subject. Most of the money therefore went to the university departments of psychology.

LEADING THE WAY

Harvard's department of psychology was headed by Dr. William McDougall. He had first arrived in Cambridge, Massachusetts, from England in 1920. He was interested in powers of the mind, and he began by training a number of assistants, or researchers. The most important of these was Joseph Banks Rhine. Rhine had studied plants as a botany student at the University of Chicago. While Rhine was at the university, he had read

At last, there was a chance for scientists to make a complete study of the powers of the mind.

Dr. McDougall's book *Body and Mind*. In his book, McDougall said that psychical research was important in order to have a full picture of how the human mind works. In 1926, Rhine gave up his botany studies. He went to Cambridge to work with Dr. McDougall. The following year, McDougall set up a psychology department at Duke University. He asked Rhine to join him there. At last, there was a chance for scientists to make a complete study of the powers of the human mind.

FIRST TESTS

Dr. Rhine began his experiments by asking people to name the order of a 52-card set of playing cards. In addition to giving the number, people were also asked to identify the color of each card (either red or black) and the suit (clubs, spades, hearts, or diamonds). Although Rhine got some interesting results, he decided that 52 was too large a number. He decided to try a more simple test.

Dr. Joseph Banks Rhine. He was one of the first scientists to make serious studies of the mysterious powers of the mind.

Karl Zener was an expert in the psychology of perception, or how we make sense of the things that we see. Rhine asked Zener to design a simple set of five playing cards. He came up with a square, a circle, a cross, a star, and a group of three wavy lines.

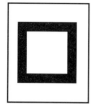

Karl Zener's designs. From left to right: a square, a circle, a cross, a star, and three wavy lines.

THE ZENER TEST

A Zener pack contains 25 cards, five of each design. Somebody guessing each card by chance would expect to get at least five correct. Each correct guess is called a "hit." If someone regularly gets more than five hits, it cannot be by chance.

Rhine tried this test on Adam J. Linzmayer, who was an economics student studying the way wealth is produced and used. Linzmayer appeared to have amazing powers. Time and time again he made nine hits out of 25. The possibility of this happening by chance was said to be 1 in 2 million!

AMAZING RESULTS

Hubert E. Pearce, Jr., a student of divinity, or the study of religious beliefs, did even better. He sat in the university library while Gaither Pratt, Rhine's assistant, sat in another building 100 yards (91 m) away. Both had set their watches so that they showed exactly the same time.

At an agreed time, Pratt took the top card off a Zener pack and put it face down, without looking at it. Pearce had to write down the card Pratt had chosen. This continued, card by card, until all 25 cards were used. Then Pratt wrote down the order. Pratt and Pearce sealed their notes in envelopes. The envelopes were then handed to Rhine.

Gaither Pratt (left) and Hubert Pearce (right) during one of Rhine's Zener tests. Pratt has put a card face down. Pearce, who is in another building, writes down what he thinks is on the card.

The results were amazing. In 12 runs through the Zener pack, Pearce scored as high as 13 hits per run. Through 30 runs—a total of 750 cards—he scored 261 hits! There was no possibility that this could have happened just by chance.

Rhine and Pratt carried out further experiments. They discovered an interesting fact. When Linzmayer and Pearce became bored with the tests, their scores dropped. Rhine decided to give them a more exciting challenge. He offered Pearce $100 for each hit. Pearce won $2,500. Every single card was correct. The chances of this happening were worked out to be almost 300 quadrillion to 1!

A NEW SCIENCE

Rhine waited several years before he published his results in a scientific journal. He had carried out 100,000 separate experiments. To make his work sound as scientific as possible, he came up with a new phrase—experiments in "extrasensory perception" (ESP). This was the first time the term had been used.

Many scientists were forced to accept the importance of Rhine's work. Dr. McDougall was given more money for his studies. He set up an Institute for Parapsychology near the Duke University campus. Rhine was made its first director. In 1937, Rhine started a magazine called the *Journal of Parapsychology*. Twenty years later he formed the Parapsychological Association. In 1969 this association was accepted as a member by the American Association for the Advancement of Science (AAAS).

. . . he came up with a new phrase—experiments in "extrasensory perception."

Other people were eager to try Rhine's Zener tests. In 1945, Dr. Gertrude Schmeidler, of City College in New York City, made an interesting discovery. She found that people who believed in ESP—she called them "sheep"—seemed to score high. Others who did not—"goats"—did not do so well.

FURTHER DEVELOPMENTS

Gradually the study of parapsychology was accepted. Around 100 universities and colleges in the U.S. now teach the subject. Other countries are carrying out scientific studies of parapsychology. Since 1978, many Chinese scientists have begun to study what they call "exceptional human body function." They claim that as many as 50 percent of children have unusual powers. However, no scientists in the West have yet been allowed to see the Chinese tests.

Military Use of ESP

In 1970, Sheila Ostrander and Lynn Schroeder wrote a book titled *Psychic Discoveries Behind the Iron Curtain*. The iron curtain was a barrier of secrecy that separated the Soviet Union, and other countries under its power, from the West.

Ostrander and Schroeder included a report from the Soviet *Maritime News* in their book. The report said that when cosmonauts (the name for Soviet astronauts) were in space, they used telepathy to communicate with each other. It went on to say that a parapsychology training system was part of the cosmonauts' training program. It seemed that the Soviets had been studying ESP for many years.

GAMES OF CAT AND MOUSE

According to Ostrander and Schroeder's book, the Soviets had also carried out ESP tests from submarines. It is possible that the U.S. Navy, too, had tried the same type of experiments. As early as 1959, French journalists had reported that telepathic messages had been sent to shore from the USS *Nautilus*. The U.S. Navy never said if this was true or not. However, news that the Soviets were taking telepathy seriously was

The USS Nautilus arriving in New York Harbor in 1956 (opposite).

34

. . . journalists reported that telepathic messages had been sent to shore from the USS Nautilus.

Three Soviet cosmonauts inside the tiny cabin of their spacecraft. According to a newspaper report, cosmonauts used telepathy to communicate with each other.

worrying for U.S. military people. If Soviet cosmonauts could really read each other's minds in space, perhaps they could also read the minds of American astronauts. If so, they would know many secrets about U.S. spaceships, as well as other secret information. Had the Soviets discovered a way of spying that could never be found out?

THE SPACE RACE

This was during a time known as the Cold War. It was not a war in the normal sense. It did not include the use of armies and guns. However, it was a time when the Soviets and Americans did not trust each other. Among other things, the two countries were trying to beat each other in what was known as the "space race." Secrecy was, therefore, very important.

Early in the 1970s, a multimillion-dollar project was set up by the American Defense Intelligence Agency (DIA). The project was called the Stargate program.

About 15 people with ESP powers worked on the program. They were all remote viewers. Their job was to help find American prisoners, Soviet submarines, and other military targets in unfriendly countries. The DIA claimed a number of successes. The remote viewers drew pictures of what the engines and insides of the Soviet submarines looked like. In 1993 it was said that the remote viewers had seen 20 tunnels being built in North Korea.

AN AMERICAN SPY

One of the people working on the Stargate program was Joe McMoneagle. He had joined the Army in 1964, at age 18, and had served in Vietnam. In 1978 he joined the Stargate program. He believed that Stargate was important for the safety of the United States.

At the start of each day, McMoneagle went to an old wooden hut and sat alone at a desk. People brought him envelopes with documents inside them. He was asked if he could provide any information about them. Sometimes there would be a photograph of somebody. McMoneagle used his remote viewing power to see where the person was to be found.

A soldier guards the entrance to one of the tunnels dug by the North Koreans. In 1993 remote viewers discovered 20 such tunnels. They had been built for a planned invasion of South Korea.

SUCCESS STORIES

Over a period of 15 years, McMoneagle said he took part in about 450 incidents. In 1980, the Central Intelligence Agency (CIA) captured a Soviet spy in South Africa. The CIA wanted to know how he had sent his information back to Russia, but the man wouldn't tell them. McMoneagle told the CIA that the man used a pocket calculator. When the calculator was examined, the CIA found that it was really a special type of radio.

McMoneagle's remote viewing powers were not only used to find out Soviet secrets. In 1978 he predicted where the space vehicle *Skylab* would fall. He did this 11 months before pieces of *Skylab* landed in the Indian Ocean and southwestern Australia on its return to Earth on July 11, 1979.

McMoneagle claimed another success in 1982. In December 1981, Brigadier General James Dozier of the U.S. Army was captured by the Italian Red Brigade. The Red Brigade was a communist terrorist

This is CIA headquarters in Langley, Virginia. The CIA spent large sums of money on psychical research and had many remote viewers working for it.

Brigadier General James Dozier speaking to the press following his rescue from the Red Brigade.

group that had begun in Milan in 1970. The following year, the group became world famous when they started to take prisoners. McMoneagle was asked to help find Dozier. He described the second-floor apartment in Padua, Italy, where the Red Brigade was holding Dozier. Italian police were able to go there and rescue him.

McMoneagle's remote viewing powers were also used to provide information about Iraq during the Persian Gulf War of 1990 to 1991. However, despite such successes, McMoneagle said that the Stargate program scored only around 25 percent success. Nevertheless, as he also said, "there is a huge percentage of intelligence systems that don't do so well."

END OF THE PROGRAM

Between 1972 and 1977, the CIA spent large sums of money on psychical research. Then, it is said, the agency gave up. In 1994, Congress ordered it to take over the Stargate program. However, in December 1995 the CIA decided that it was a waste of money and closed it down.

But, as Senator Claiborne Pell of Rhode Island put it: "If the CIA is not interested, that's their business. I am convinced [certain] that we should continue the research." And reports suggest that the Russians are still carrying out tests using ESP.

39

Is There an Explanation?

There have now been many studies of ESP. But have any of them been able to explain these mysterious powers?

Over the years, scientists have had to accept that experiments in ESP have produced real results. However, ESP researchers have had to be very careful to make their experiments as scientific as possible. They have to be sure that signals cannot pass from one person to another.

THE COUNTING HORSE

Many years ago there was a famous horse called "Clever Hans." Some people claimed that this horse could count. The horse would tap its hoof until it reached the right answer. It was later discovered that, in fact, the horse's owner moved ever so slightly every time Hans reached the right number. His owner claimed that he did not know he was making any signals. However, when Hans sensed the movement, he stopped tapping his hoof.

To stop this type of accidental signaling, most people testing the powers of ESP are kept apart from one another. They are put in separate rooms, with no scientifically known way of contacting each other. That is why objects or pictures that are to be seen are chosen by computers. This avoids human contact.

A young psychic "looks" inside two sealed envelopes during an ESP test. (opposite). As yet, there appears to be no explanation for such powers.

Perhaps ESP really is our sixth sense. But how does this sixth sense work?

"Clever Hans" and his owner in 1904. Hans was said to have ESP until it was found that his owner was, in fact, accidentally showing the horse what to do.

BASIC SENSES

Most scientists understand the basics of how our five senses—hearing, touch, taste, smell, and sight—work. Sound is carried by vibrations in the air, or through liquids or solids. Touch is a matter of physical pressure. Nerves in the body send messages to the brain when they feel pressure. Even the lightest of touches can be felt. The chemicals that produce tastes or smells "lock on" to special sensitive areas in the mouth, or at the back of the nose. Each chemical behaves something like a tiny spacecraft connecting with a docking module. The sensitive areas then send a message to the brain. This is one of the reasons why some people smell and taste things differently.

Many things can affect the sensitive areas of the body. For example, when we have a bad cold, the sensitive areas in the nose become less sensitive to smells. Therefore, an onion will have no smell. It will just taste sweet.

Sight works in still another way. Light from objects shines into our eyes. It hits special cells at the back of the eyes, and these send messages to the brain. At one time, ESP was sometimes known as "second sight." Scientists have wondered if ESP could be related in some way to normal sight.

LIGHT CONNECTIONS

Light is only a small part of a wide range of vibrations called electromagnetic radiation. These vibrations are not like sound. They do not need air or any solid or liquid to carry them from one place to another. However, like sound they have wavelength. Imagine a straight piece of string. Then imagine the piece of string with wiggles in it like a snake. The distance between the top of one wiggle, where the vibration is greatest, and the next is a wavelength.

For centuries, scientists believed that these vibrations must be carried by something. They thought this something might be called the "ether." This was thought to be colorless and tasteless. It had to be all around us and also throughout space. However, a number of clever experiments finally proved that there was no such thing as the ether in physics.

The wavelengths of electromagnetic radiation range from miles to distances that are so small they are hard to imagine. The longest wavelengths are used in radio. Shorter waves are used in television.

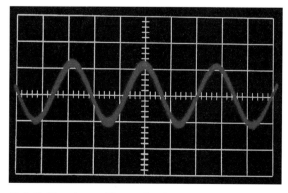

Both light and sound have what is called a wavelength. This illustration shows what a wavelength looks like.

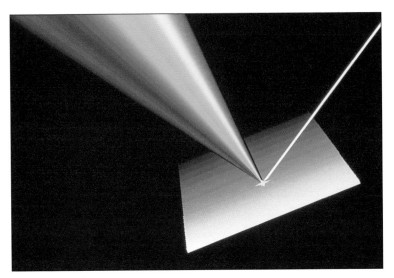

White light consists of many colors. If a beam of light passes through glass it bends. Then, the different colors can be seen. This image was made on a computer.

Then, slightly shorter still, are the microwaves that are used in the ovens. Infrared heat waves have an even shorter wavelength than microwaves. If an object is heated enough, it begins to give off light. First, the light is red. Then, the object gives out shorter wavelengths—colored yellow, blue, and violet. These colors blend together until the object is white-hot. When we see light as one color, it actually contains all these colors.

Ultraviolet radiation is even shorter in wavelength than infrared heat waves. The human eye cannot see it—although some other animals, such as insects, can. Beyond the ultraviolet come X rays. Then come gamma rays, which are even shorter than X rays.

INVISIBLE LIGHT

Human eyes can see only the tiny range of light wavelengths from red through violet. But ESP researchers have wondered if the human brain can send out, and receive, longer wavelength signals. To test this, they have put people inside Faraday cages. Michael Faraday was one of the greatest scientists of the 19th century. He discovered many important facts about electricity and magnetism. Faraday cages are metal structures that stop radio waves from passing through them. They act like the outer weave of metal wires around a television cable. However, people can still receive messages by ESP inside a Faraday cage.

Nevertheless, people cannot send out light signals. When we see a person, we see light reflected from, or shining off, them. They are not sending light to our eyes. Therefore, it seems unlikely they could send signals of longer, or shorter, wavelengths.

BRAIN ACTIVITY

Making electromagnetic radiation requires a lot of energy. Think of the amount of heat energy that

A Faraday cage in Professor John Hasted's laboratory at Birkbeck College in London.

needs to be put into an object to make it white-hot. People who can receive telepathic messages, or use remote viewing, become tired when they use their powers. But this tiredness is mental, rather than physical.

Scientists have been unable to find any proof of electromagnetic energy being produced in ESP tests. But there is evidence that the brain seems to work in an unusual way. For example, when Ingo Swann drew his pictures by remote viewing, his brain waves changed shape.

45

A SIXTH SENSE?

Even today, there is a lot that scientists do not understand about the human brain. Perhaps ESP really is our sixth sense. But how does this sixth sense work?

Scientists only know about things that they can measure. Until they understood how smell and taste worked, they had no way of measuring the strength of a smell. Now, equipment has been made that can measure the amounts of smelly substances in the air. Sniffer machines at airports are used to find drugs and explosives. Perhaps, some day, it will be possible to build a machine that can measure ESP—in the same way that we are able to receive radio and television broadcasts.

A scientist looks at a man's brain waves. A picture of the brain is shown on the screen. It has been found that brain waves change their shape during remote viewing tests.

LOOKING TO THE FUTURE

People who have studied ESP can only put forward their ideas. Scientists know about electricity, gravity, electromagnetic radiation, and magnetism. These are the forces that surround the human body. But ESP experts suggest that there is another force. This is a force that causes psychic, rather than physical, events to happen. However, no one has yet been able to find any scientific way of proving that such a force exists. But who can tell what the future may bring?

Glossary

clairvoyance The ability to "see" into the future. From the French word, meaning "clear seeing."

cosmos Garden plants of the family Asteraceae, which consists of around 20 species. The common garden cosmos is *Cosmos bipinnatus*. Cosmos also means the universe.

destination A place to which someone or something is going or being sent.

docking module Part of a spaceship that leaves the main part of a spacecraft to carry out specific tasks. It then docks with, or rejoins, the spacecraft.

electromagnetic radiation Energy in the form of electric and magnetic (electromagnetic) waves. For example, radio waves, infrared waves, microwaves, visible light, ultraviolet, X rays, and gamma rays.

extrasensory perception (ESP) Unexplained powers of the mind. People with such powers seem to make use of something other than the five senses of sight, touch, hearing, taste, and smell.

laboratory A room designed for scientific experiments and research.

magnetism The invisible pushing and pulling forces of a magnet.

parapsychology The study of happenings that cannot be explained by normal science.

physics The scientific study of natural forces, such as light, heat, sound, electricity, and magnetism.

psychic A person who claims to be able to see into the future, or who has other unexplained powers.

psychokinesis (PK) The ability to make objects move using only the power of the mind.

psychology The scientific study of the human mind and how it affects human behavior.

remote viewing A type of ESP in which a person "sends" his or her mind to look at something that cannot be seen from where the person is sitting or standing.

researchers People making a serious, detailed study of something, usually for scientific purposes.

telepathy Mind reading, or the sending of thoughts from one person's mind to another.

ultraviolet radiation A type of electromagnetic radiation with an extremely short wavelength.

vibrations A slight, continuous shuddering or shaking movement.

X ray An electromagnetic ray that can pass through most materials apart from metal and bone. X rays are used to produce photographic images of anything consisting of metal or bone.

Index

Further Reading

Arvey, Michael. *ESP: Opposing Viewpoints*. Greenhaven, 1989
Green, Carl R., and William R. Sanford. *Mysterious Mind Powers*. Enslow,
1993
Larsen, Anita. *Psychic Sleuths: How Psychic Information Is Used to Solve Crimes*.
Silver Burdett Press, 1994
Skurzynski, Gloria. *Waves: The Invisible Universe*. National Geographic, 1996